Memento

MY LIFE IN STORIES

Michael McQueen

CHRONICLE BOOKS

SAN FRANCISCO

First published in the United States in 2010 by Chronicle Books LLC.

Text copyright © 2008 by Michael McQueen.
Originally published in Australia in 2008 by Park Street Press,
under the title *Memento: The Gift of a Lifetime*.
Illustrations copyright © 2010 by Josée Bisaillon.

ISBN: 978-0-8118-7375-8

Manufactured in China.

Designed by Jennifer Tolo Pierce.
Illustration by Josée Bisaillon.

10 9 8 7 6 5 4 3 2 1

Chronicle Books LLC
680 Second Street
San Francisco, California 94107

www.chroniclebooks.com

{ CONTENTS }

FOREWORD

When I was twenty-two, my world was turned upside down. It was Monday, October 11, and I had called my dad in the morning just to catch up. We talked about normal things: the weather, the weekend, and how work was going. Our conversation was neither significant nor memorable and it finished with a promise that I would drop in to see him and Mom for dinner that evening.

Little did I know that this was a promise I would never be able to keep.

Later that morning I received a phone call I will never forget. His voice trembling, my older brother urged me to drop whatever I was doing and get to the hospital as soon as I could. He simply said that Dad had collapsed at home, and warned that things did not look good.

During the three hours it took me to drive to the hospital, I played out every possible scenario in my mind. By the time I arrived, I had reassured myself that it was probably nothing and had decided not to get worried before I knew more about the situation.

But when I got to the hospital, the look on the nurse's face made it clear that my life was about to change forever. The doctors said it was "a massive heart attack without warning." That was the only explanation we got.

And with that, my closest mentor and friend was gone forever.

In the days and weeks that followed, my family and I faced the heartbreaking task of sorting through my father's belongings. As we sifted through trinkets, photos, and tokens of his life, we came across something that made my heart leap the moment I saw it. There, in the bottom drawer of his desk, was a well-worn notebook that I had forgotten even existed.

I recognized this book instantly as the gift I had given Dad for Father's Day the previous year. Armed with a list of questions, I had somewhat sheepishly asked him to write down stories and experiences from his life that had never come up in conversation.

At the time I had no idea just how significant this simple request would be.

As I sat there 14 months later, reading through the stories and experiences that he had recorded, I found myself captivated by how much I didn't know about my father and his life. I was struck by the things that were important to him but had gone unspoken, and also by how much we had in common.

In numerous conversations over the next few months, I found myself recounting to others the experience of both finding and reading the notebook my father had left behind. I was amazed at how the story struck a chord with so many people. Everyone, it seemed, had a loved one whom they wished had filled out a similar book.

And so the idea for *Memento* was born.

It all started with a simple question I e-mailed to everyone in my contact list: *What do you wish you could ask a loved one who is no longer alive?* The response was overwhelming . . . everyone I e-mailed had long lists of questions they wish they could have asked a parent, a grandparent, a mentor, a partner, or a son or daughter before it was too late.

In my work as a professional speaker, I meet with tens of thousands of people each year from every conceivable background, age, demographic, and culture. Interestingly, I have found that the theme of connecting generations is one that resonates across the spectrum—perhaps most surprisingly with young people. Having worked with over 80,000 students, I can attest to the fact that young people today are searching for a meaningful connection with their family heritage more than ever before.

While this may come as a shock to many parents and grandparents, I would suggest that the reason for such a yearning is clear—this younger generation has grown up in an era that doesn't value the past. After all, not that long ago the process of "passing down" through the generations was at the core of our social fabric. Culture developed, history was preserved, craftsmanship was taught, and wisdom was bestowed through the stories passed down from father to son, mother to daughter, grandparent to grandchild. Whether around the campfire, the watering hole, or the dinner table, our elders showed us how the world worked and the meaning of our place within it.

In just one short century, though, so much has changed. We have shifted from a "built-to-last" society to a "quick-fix" culture. We crave the newest cars and fastest computers, while anything deemed to be dated, old, and "yesterday" is simply disregarded or disposed. Our obsession with progress is typified by the modern-day doctrine that everything old is "bad" and everything new is "good."

The link between generations is under increasing threat and young people sense it. In homes across the Western world, a dramatic role reversal is occurring: for the first time, it is the "tech-savvy" *younger* generation teaching their *elders* how the world works.

While it is true that older generations were raised in a vastly different time, it is equally true that the principles, values, and experiences that guided and shaped their lives are as relevant and applicable today as they were in centuries past. I suspect that the advice and comfort to be found in the wisdom of older generations is needed even more than younger people recognize (or are willing to openly admit).

My own experience can attest to this. In the years since my father died, I have often gone back to his journal to find guidance, advice, and hope.

I can learn from his mistakes and feel empowered by his successes. In this way his journal has become more than the musings of a sentimental parent—this book and the stories it contains are my father's legacy.

Each day we create our legacy. We make memories, learn lessons, collect experiences, and grow relationships that become the richly woven fabric of our life.

While a fortunate few have a library or the wing of a hospital named in their honor, and others can point to streets, suburbs or even comets that bear their name, surely the most meaningful legacy we can leave is not in the accomplishments we accrue but in the lives we touch—especially when they belong to our family.

Memento is designed to be a family keepsake that will live on well beyond your years. It is an ideal way for you to record the stories of life that you have not yet had the opportunity to share.

The purpose of this book is to help you capture the memories and moments that have defined and shaped your life. Some of the questions will draw out the deep and the profound, others simply aim to expose the fun, daring, and downright embarrassing moments of life. Make this an honest account of your life—one that includes both your successes *and* your failures.

Ultimately, my hope is that this book will become an heirloom for your family in the way my father's journal has for mine. May it not only bear witness to your life and times, but act as a source of comfort, inspiration, and humor for the generations to come. In this way, the stories you record in the following pages could make all the difference to the next generation as they face the same challenges, situations, and circumstances you yourself have encountered.

Naturally, something this significant doesn't come without a price. It will require you to invest two of your most valuable assets: your time and your memories. I trust that you will see this as a worthwhile investment and that your children's children will be glad you did too!

Warmest regards,

Michael McQueen
Sydney, Australia

This life belongs to:

....

{ PERSONAL TIMELINE }

birth

today

N°. 1

MY YOUNGER YEARS

What was the house you grew up in like? How would you describe it?
Was there a place in it that was special for you?

When you were growing up, did you move often as a family?
How did you feel about that?

If you had siblings growing up, did you feel that you were all treated equally by your parents?
How did you feel about this?

"Who of us is mature enough
for offspring before offspring themselves
arrive? The value of marriage is not
that adults produce children, but that
children produce adults."

PETER DE VRIES

If you had brothers and sisters, what do you remember about growing up with them?
To whom were you closest?

What was your favorite childhood toy? What was so special about it?
Did you have any hobbies as a child? If so, what were they?

"A dog is the only thing on earth
that loves you more than he loves himself."

JOSH BILLINGS

Did you grow up owning pets? If so, what do you remember about them?

How wealthy or poor was your family when you were growing up?
In what ways did this impact home life and your approach to money as an adult?

How much allowance did you get when you were young
and on what did you spend it?

How much did "the basics" (bread, milk, etc.) cost when you were young?

Do you remember going to a funeral as a child?
In what ways did this affect you and what can you remember about it?

Did your family own a TV when you were growing up?
If so, what do you remember watching?

In 1959, NBC first brought
full color broadcasting to television
viewers around the world with its
hit Western series *Bonanza*.

When you were younger, was there any food you didn't like and refused to eat?
How did your parents respond? Do you eat it now? If so, what changed?

Did you ever get lost as a child?
Do you remember where you were and how that felt?

Did you ever have imaginary friends or companions? Can you describe them?

Would you describe your family as close, as you were growing up?
What was that like for you?

"A wise man should consider
that health is the greatest of human blessings,
and learn how by his own thought to derive
benefit from his illnesses."

HIPPOCRATES

Did you have any illnesses or health problems as a child?
How did these affect you at the time and do you remember how your family reacted?

What did your family normally do on weekends?

Do you have any special memories of things you did on a regular basis?

What notable events do you remember going to as a younger child?
What made them memorable?

Did you ever pray as a young child? If so, was it instinctive or did someone teach or encourage you to?
Do you remember what you prayed for?

"Prayer begins where human capacity ends."

MARIAN ANDERSON

What do you remember about your first job? How much did you get paid?
How did it influence your work ethic?

....

....

....

....

....

....

....

....

....

....

....

....

....

....

....

....

Who were your friends at school? Do you still keep in touch with them?
Why or why not?

From 1892 to 1954,
over twelve million immigrants
entered the United States through the
Ellis Island Immigration Center
in New York Harbor.

If you emigrated as a child, what was that like for you?

What do you remember thinking or feeling when you arrived here?

What was your favorite subject at school? Why this subject?

Which schools did you go to? How would you describe your experience of school?

Which of your school teachers had the greatest impact on you?
What was most significant about them?

"Teachers do more than impart
facts and figures—they inspire and encourage
students and instill a true desire to learn.
That's a fine art in itself."

SONNY PERDUE

"The difference between school
and life? In school, you're taught a lesson
and then given a test. In life, you're given
a test that teaches you a lesson."

TOM BODETT

What sort of student were you at school?
Did you ever fail a subject and if so, what were the consequences?

What were some of the fads that you most remember from your school days?
Did you get involved in them?

In 1957, the hula hoop
was reinvented by Richard Knerr and
Arthur Melin, founders of the Wham-O
toy company. After the hoop was released
in 1958, Wham-O sold over 100 million
in two years.

What was the most rebellious thing you did as a teenager?

Would you do it again if you could relive your teenage years?

What was your father's occupation? Did his work interest you at all?

What was your mother's occupation? Did her work interest you at all?

How did your parents' work affect life at home?

In 1952, the 5 best-selling fiction books were:

The Caine Mutiny—HERMAN WOUK

The Silver Chalice—THOMAS B. COSTAIN

East of Eden—JOHN STEINBECK

Giant—EDNA FERBER

Steamboat Gothic—FRANCES PARKINSON KEYES

Did you enjoy reading when you were younger?
If so, what books do you remember liking the most?

When you were younger, did your family have a regular place for summer vacations?
If so, what is your fondest memory of those vacations?

What kind of car did your family have when you were growing up?
Do you remember being embarrassed by it or proud of it at the time?

"To me, there is no greater act of courage than being the one who kisses first."

JANEANE GAROFALO

What can you remember about your first kiss? Who was it with and where were you?

As a teenager, did you ever feel like you didn't fit in? How did that affect you?

What is the kindest and most considerate thing you ever did for your parents?

What do you remember about your first date? Tell all . . .

"Nothing defines humans better than their willingness to do irrational things in the pursuit of phenomenally unlikely payoffs. This is the principle behind lotteries, dating, and religion."

SCOTT ADAMS, AMERICAN CARTOONIST

What was the most embarrassing thing you did to get the attention
of someone you wanted to date?

At what age did you move out of your parents' home?
How do you remember feeling at the time?

How old were you when you met your spouse or partner?

What do you remember of that experience and what attracted you to him or her?

....

....

....

....

....

....

....

....

....

....

....

....

....

....

....

....

Was there a time that you realized he or she was "the one" for you?
How did you know that?

"A real soul mate is the one you are married to."

J.R.R. TOLKIEN

What can you remember about where and how you proposed to him or her,
or where and how you were proposed to?

Did you ever feel that you made a mistake in choosing the person you married?
If so, how did you respond to this?

What was your wedding day like? How did you feel?
Did anything go significantly wrong?

Where did you go for your honeymoon? Share what that was like . . .

"Happiness consists of living each day
as if it were the first day of your honeymoon
and the last day of your vacation."

ANONYMOUS

Where did you first live when you got married? What was your first home like?

At what point, if any, did you start talking about having children?
How many did you plan on having?

In 1960, the average house price
in America was $16,500, which represented
approximately 2.9 times the annual wage.
However, by 2006, average prices had risen
to over $305,000, which was 6.3 times
the annual wage.

When you bought your first house, how much did it cost?
Where was it and how did owning it make you feel?

MY FAMILY HERITAGE

great-grandfather

great-grandmother

great-grandfather

great-grandmother

grandfather

grandmother

great-grandfather

great-grandmother

great-grandfather

great-grandmother

grandfather

grandmother

{ FAMILY TREE }

father

mother

me

Did your family regularly get together with extended family?
What were those occasions like and how did you all get along?

"Like all the best families,
we have our share of eccentricities,
of impetuous and wayward youngsters,
and of family disagreements."

QUEEN ELIZABETH II

What religious influences, if any, were there on you from your family?

Is there anyone in your family history that has been famous, infamous,
or achieved something extraordinary?

What are your ancestral countries of origin? Have you ever traveled there or met distant relatives? If so, describe that experience.

How openly did your family embrace diversity?
In what ways has this shaped your attitudes toward others?

"Grandmothers are the people
who take delight in hearing babies
breathing into the telephone."

PAM BROWN

What do you remember about your grandparents?

How would you describe your parents' relationship and its impact on you?

Who of your extended family were particularly important to you?
What was so significant about them?

WHAT I VALUE & BELIEVE

Have you ever felt so passionate about something that you were moved to act?
What did you do?

Can you remember a time when you helped someone in need?
What did that mean to you?

Do you remember any experiences in your life that you would describe as particularly spiritual?
How did they affect you?

Have you ever felt that you have a specific purpose or reason for being alive?
If so, how would you describe it?

"A truly good book teaches me
better than to read it. I must soon lay it down,
and commence living on its hint. What I began
by reading, I must finish by acting."

HENRY DAVID THOREAU

Is there a book or author who has significantly challenged or influenced your view of the world?
If so, how?

Would you describe yourself as a naturally optimistic or pessimistic person?
How does this affect your everyday life?

"Optimism is the foundation of courage."

NICHOLAS MURRAY BUTLER

Have you ever had a near-death experience or seriously feared for your life?
How did this influence your perspective on living?

If you had a month left to live, what would you do?

"I don't know the key to success,
but the key to failure is to try to please everyone."

BILL COSBY

How do you define success? Has this definition changed over time?

How would you describe your political persuasion?
Who or what has influenced this most significantly?

What is your view on the importance of money? What shaped this view?

What is your favorite sport? Why this one?
What game or event was the most memorable to you?

The 2008 Super Bowl was the most-watched sporting match ever with an astonishing 97 million viewers. The only TV program in American history to have attracted more viewers was the 1983 finale of the hit series *M*A*S*H*.

Have you ever experimented with drugs? How do you feel about that in retrospect?

When and how were you taught about sex? Do you think this prepared you well for adult life?
If not, what would you have done differently?

According to the 2001 Encyclopedia
Britannica Book of the Year, there are over
10,000 distinct religions worldwide.

Do you believe in a higher power? What has influenced this view?

*What significant events have influenced the way you view yourself
or the world around you?*

Have you ever stolen anything? What was it and how did you feel afterward?

How were you disciplined as a child and do you think that was effective and fair?

"Discipline doesn't break
a child's spirit half as often as the lack
of it breaks a parent's heart."

ANONYMOUS

Would you describe yourself as community minded?
If so, how have you expressed that throughout your life?

How do you feel about facing death? What do you think happens after we die?

"Miracles are not contrary
to nature, but only contrary to what
we know about nature."

SAINT AUGUSTINE

Do you believe in miracles? Why?

N°. 4

WHAT I HAVE LEARNED

ABOUT MYSELF & THE WORLD

How would you describe your personality? How has this changed over time?

Can you describe the best gift you ever received? What about the worst?

How do you most like to spend a free day? Do you prefer doing things alone or with others?

"The end of labor is to gain leisure."

ARISTOTLE

How are you like your father and mother?
In what ways have you specifically tried to be different?

What, in your opinion, makes a successful marriage?

If your marriage didn't work out as you had planned, what happened?
How did you react?

If you have ever gone through a divorce or separation, how did it affect you and how did you come to that decision? At what point, if ever, did you feel ready for another relationship and how did you know you were ready?

What is the most disgusting thing you have ever eaten?

Did you ever have a nickname? How did that come about?
Did you ever wish you could change it?

The first fully automatic mobile phone
was released in 1956 by Swedish company
Ericsson. Weighing as much as a bag of cement,
these early phones heralded a new age
in wireless communication.

What technology has changed life for you the most since you were younger?
How do you feel about these changes?

Describe your most memorable New Year's Eve experiences.

What is the most unusual or bizarre thing you have ever seen?

What is your favorite movie and why?

In terms of box office earnings, the 10 most popular movies of all time in the United States are:

1. *Titanic*, 1997

2. *The Dark Knight*, 2008

3. *Star Wars*, 1977

4. *Shrek 2*, 2004

5. *E.T.: The Extra-Terrestrial*, 1982

6. *Star Wars:* Episode I *The Phantom Menace*, 1999

7. *Pirates of the Carribbean: Dead Man's Chest*, 2006

8. *Spider-Man*, 2002

9. *Star Wars:* Episode III *Revenge of the Sith*, 2005

10. *The Lord of the Rings: The Return of the King*, 2003

When you became a parent, do you remember how that felt?
Did your reaction surprise you?

What are some of your most vivid memories of your children as they were growing up?

If you had the chance, is there anything you would change about the way
you raised your children?

Do you remember something said to you that was so hurtful it has remained with you?
Who said it and how did it make you feel?

"A real friend is one who walks in
when the rest of the world walks out."

WALTER WINCHELL

They say a fortunate person has a handful of trusted friends at the end of his or her life.
Who would be on your list? What do you think makes a good friend?

Have you ever been involved in a physical fight or tried to stop one?

Have you ever fought any addictions in your life? How did that affect you?
Any lessons you could share?

Have you ever traveled overseas?

What was your favorite place and how has travel shaped your view of the world?

"The wise man travels to discover himself."

JAMES RUSSELL LOWELL

When do you remember being most afraid in your life? How did you cope?

If you had to choose a "last meal," what would it be? Why?

Have there been any times when you were under financial stress?
How did you feel and what did you learn from the experience?

Who is the most famous person you have ever met?
What was your impression of him or her?

Computers in the 1960s were huge,
heavy machines that took up entire rooms
in air-conditioned buildings. In contrast,
some modern day wristwatches are more
powerful than the combined computer
power used in the entire Apollo 11
moon landing mission.

Do you remember the first time you used a computer?
What was your first impression?

Can you remember the best practical joke you ever played on someone or participated in?
What was the outcome?

....

....

....

....

....

....

....

....

....

....

....

....

....

....

....

....

"April 1. This is the day upon which
we are reminded of what we are on the
other three-hundred and sixty-four."

MARK TWAIN

When do you remember being most angry in your life?
What caused you to react so strongly?

Can you describe where you were when man walked on the moon, JFK was assassinated,
Princess Diana died, and the attacks of September 11 happened?

"Not all those who wander are lost."

J.R.R. TOLKIEN

What is the most adventurous thing you have ever done?

How would you describe the experience of being a grandparent?
In what ways is it different from being a parent?

What is your most vivid Thanksgiving or holiday memory?

According to *Rolling Stone* magazine,
the 5 greatest songs of all time are:

1. "Like a Rolling Stone"– BOB DYLAN

2. "Satisfaction"– THE ROLLING STONES

3. "Imagine"– JOHN LENNON

4. "What's Going On"– MARVIN GAYE

5. "Respect"– ARETHA FRANKLIN

What is your favorite song?

Does it remind you of anything or anyone specifically and how do you feel when you hear it?

N°. 5

MY HOPES & DREAMS

Were there any talents and skills that your parents actively fostered in you as you were growing up?
If so, what were they and how important was your parents' encouragement at the time?

"Correction does much,
but encouragement does more."

GOETHE

Do you remember what you wanted to be "when you grew up"?

Can you imagine pursuing that path now in hindsight? What might have been different if you had?

Did you learn to play a musical instrument when you were younger? If so, what was it?
How would you rate your musical abilities? Is there any instrument you wish you had learnt?

"There is nothing wrong with making a mistake—as long as you don't follow it up with encores."

ANONYMOUS

What is your greatest regret in life? What would you do differently if you had the chance?

What are your children's names?
Why did you name your children the way you did?

As a parent, what hopes and dreams did you have for your children
when they were younger?

What has been the proudest moment of your life?

Has there been there a specific project of which you were particularly proud? What was it?

"All the things we achieve
are things we have first of all imagined
and then made happen."

DAVID MALOUF

If you were to ever write a book, what would it be about and what would you call it?

What opportunities have you "missed" in life and wished you had taken?
What held you back?

In his book *Unforgettable Places to See Before You Die*, Steven Davey lists his top 5 must-see destinations:

Angkor Wat, CAMBODIA

Saint Petersburg, RUSSIA

La Habana, CUBA

Wat Phra Kaeo, THAILAND

Grand Canyon, UNITED STATES

What would be on your list of places around the world that you hope to one day visit?

If you could travel through time to any period of history, when would it be and why?

Have you ever started your own business or wished you had? What kind of business?

Have you kept a journal or diary over the years? If so, do you still have them?

"People who keep journals have life twice."

JESSAMYN WEST

If you could have a conversation with anyone living or dead, who would it be?
What would you talk about?

What would you like people to say about you at your funeral?

"When you can think of yesterday
without regret and tomorrow without fear,
you are near contentment."

ANONYMOUS

What would you most like to see change in the world?

If you could, which five minutes would you like to live over again?

{ NOTES }